AI WEIWEI

MANIFESTO

WITHOUT BORDERS

PalmArtPress

The following text is based on the transcription of personal audio recordings, exclusive sources, and quotations from the author, all translated from Chinese into German by Eva Schestag. This text was then translated from German into English by Catharine J. Nicely and Irina Kogan.

CONTENT

WHY I AM WRITING THIS BOOK

Preface

I have given many interviews in my life—probably several hundred. But such question-and-answer conversations are often fragmented and tied to the fleeting situations. They always capture only segments of reality.

A book, in contrast, offers the opportunity to circle around ideas and present them differently in all their complexity. That is why I want to let the reader witness how such thoughts arise and how they grow into *actions*. Making this process visible is important to me.

Without thoughts
I am a blank page
—for now.
This means
my present Self
does not (yet) exist.

That's why I have to,
first and foremost, find myself.
And then—once I have
managed to do so—tell
the reader *who* I am.
And how I found myself.

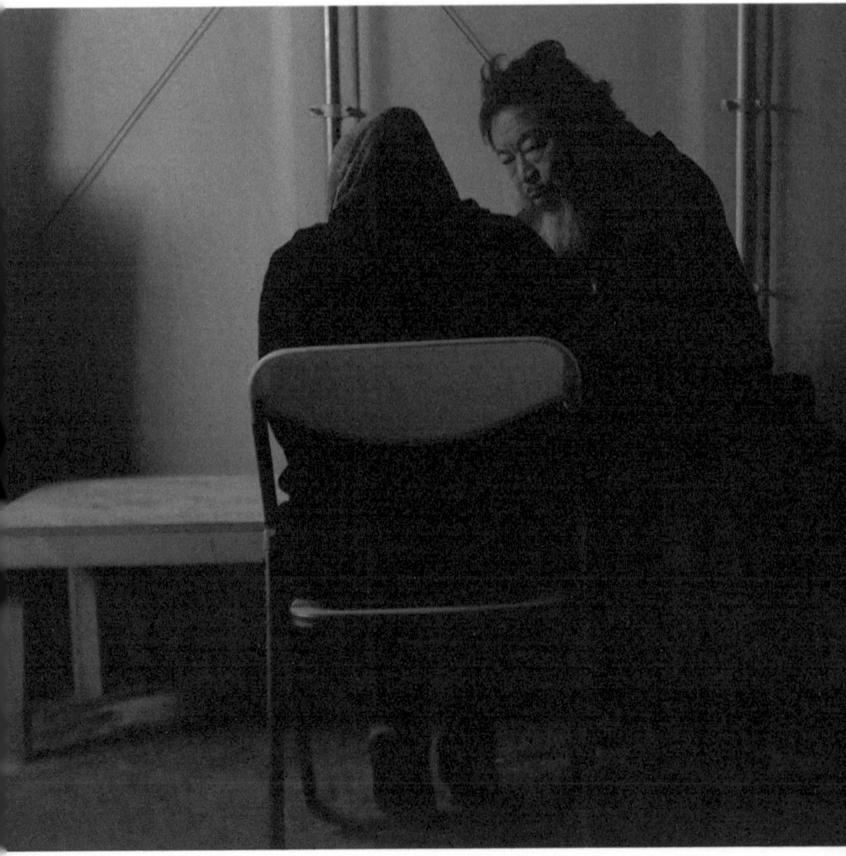

The path leads
through others,
through an interest
in them.

With *Human Flow*, I made a film about the global refugee movement.

This work profoundly shaped me, even though I had already addressed aspects of the so-called "refugee question" earlier in my career—which I also want to share.

Ultimately, I came to understand that we are *all* part of a refugee cosmos—either because we were once refugees ourselves or because we *made* others into refugees—both victims and perpetrators at the same time.

This direct connection is undeniable. Has it not been our lack of self-understanding, combined with a sense of superiority that has contributed to the refugee crisis?

The self-righteous assumption that we are fundamentally different from "them" is part of the catastrophe.

This is also why I want to let my thoughts wander with this book: What is the relationship between individuals—whether they are refugees or "locals"?

Humanity is not an abstract concept. It becomes truly meaningful and tangible precisely when it begins to disappear.

In any given region, when people
are harmed, all are,
in a sense, wounded.

And with that, we are already in the midst of a story that is far greater than just my own.

MY ORIGINS

Chapter 1.

My earliest memory is a sentence from my father: "We have to move on." At the time, we were already in a very remote place, far in the west of China.

The year I was born, my father, the poet Ai Qing, became a victim of a political purge called the "Anti-Rightist Campaign"; he was imprisoned and later exiled. He was forced to leave Beijing and was forbidden to write a single line for twenty years.

The region to which we had been forcibly relocated was mainly inhabited by Uyghurs. At some point, I heard that phrase: "We have to move on—and we have to move now." Into even greater distance, into even greater uncertainty. And yet, we already had nothing, not even a bed.

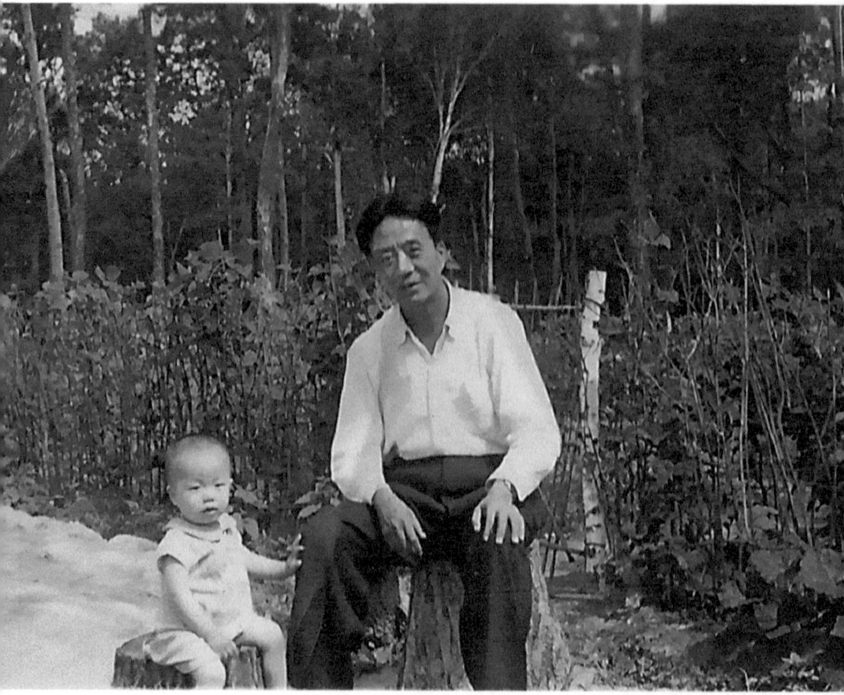

All we could take on this renewed, involuntary move were merely blankets—and coal. We expected it be extremely cold at the other place and feared there would be nothing there to warm ourselves up with. I remember how I was sitting on a small heap of coal on the transport wagon, just like that.

This is what it means to have to leave a place that, for all of its strangeness and inhospitable nature, had at least become somewhat familiar, and move on again into the unknown. And to own nothing, or almost nothing. A way, but not a way out.

A kind of non-situation or half-existence. For, owning nothing means that one has nothing to care for or fight over—which, for better or worse, makes up part of one's life.

I still wonder about that state–how one endures such a form of nakedness.

To this day, whenever I hear the words “family” or “home,” I still see that rickety wagon and myself as a child, sitting lost on that heap of coal.

A real home could never exist under such conditions. And indeed, even in the village where we arrived, the persecution and discrimination continued. Today, it would be called: “forced migration,” but that sounds much too academic. Reality was this: My father was harassed, insulted and beaten in the street. Some people even poured dirt and ink over his head.

He had to do the hardest, menial work, like cleaning primitive public toilets. In those rural areas there was no toilet paper or running water, just mud and sand.

That hostile world and curses of the village people still remain very present in my memory. This early experience of daily humiliation left a deep mark on me. Perhaps that's why I know so well what it feels like to be a foreigner—to be regarded by those around you, by society, as a danger that must be combated.

And yet, at that time, we did not see ourselves as *refugees*—certainly not with any kind of romantic or heroic connotation. We were simply called "enemies of the state" or "enemies of the people."

We had no status at all, and even this lack of status could still be made worse.

But above all: we had no voice to say *who* we were. That is something that displaced people of today also suffer; this too is a universal experience.

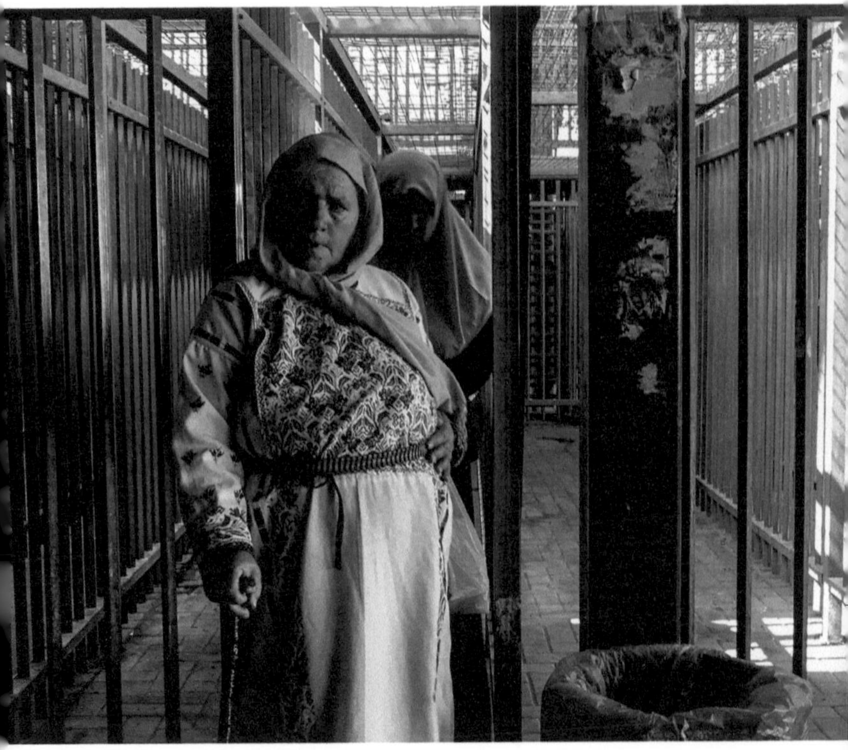

What is baffling—though perhaps following a dark kind of logic—is how all these mechanisms of exclusion have remained the same, regardless of time and place. First, a fellow human is depicted as an outsider, as something irregular. From there, it is only a short step to perceiving them as a danger, as a threat to all the supposedly "normal" people.

How little it takes for a majority to be persuaded that you don't belong to it! Yet, the figure of the ominous stranger is a fiction that someone previously had to devise.

And this someone could be *anyone*—you just as well as me.

We must keep reminding ourselves of this, so as not to fall into that very trap.

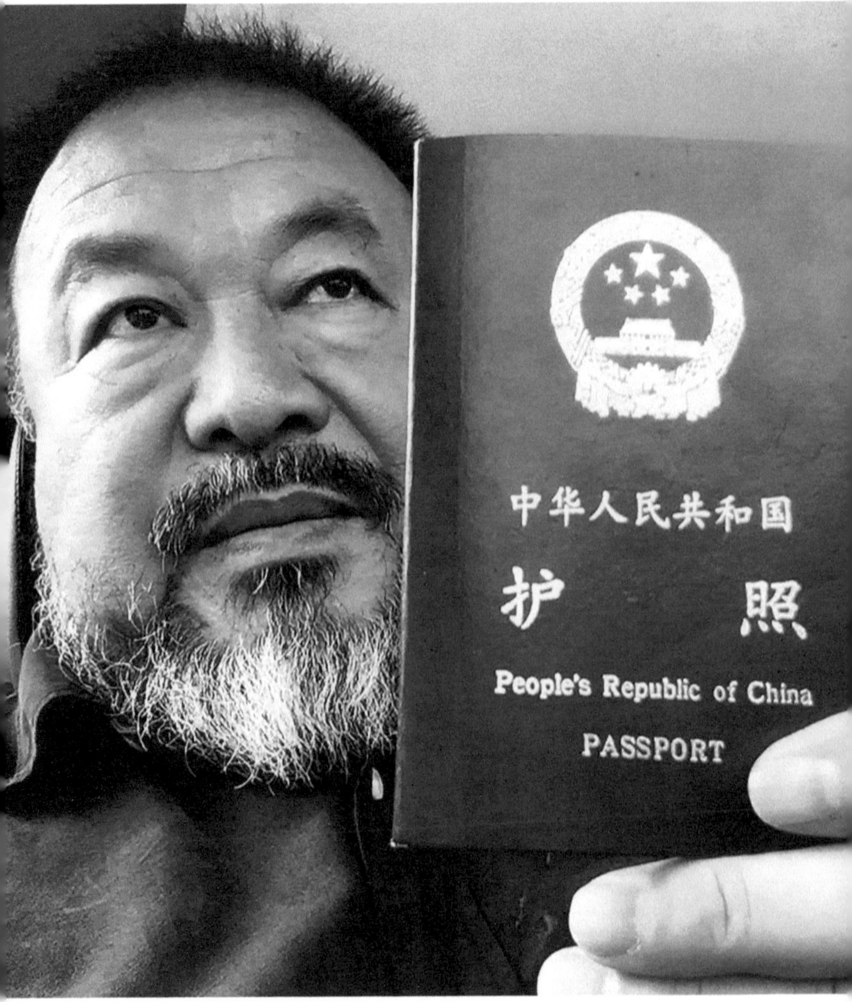

中华人民共和国
护 照
People's Republic of China
PASSPORT

Exclusion is the first
and foremost element
of hatred in this world—
and also its product.

No one is immune to it—neither as victim nor as perpetrator.

Such hatred can strike any given human being, through injury or defamation. First, the individual loses their reputation, then their very existence. They are effectively cut off from society and, in many cases, later even from life itself. Help and solidarity in such circumstances are rarer than precious gems.

Anyone who helps in such a situation—or even just shows compassion—risks being seen as a traitor, someone who, in turn, should be cast out.

This is an age-old mechanism, yet it is not *simply* atavistic. Even in modern life, in the everyday politics of today's democracies, it appears and has real impact:

A politician who expresses too much solidarity with the fate of refugees could, under certain circumstances, represent a latent threat to colleagues who fear losing voters' sympathy.

I experienced all of this more or less from birth until about my twentieth birthday. It was only then that my father was rehabilitated. Afterward, we were allowed to move back to Beijing. But what had happened before would shape me for the rest of my life. Once a human being has become a refugee, they remain one forever—even if they are later allowed to be "integrated" and their circumstances improve.

More than that: Such positive changes may even intensify the existential sense of being a stranger. At least that was my experience.

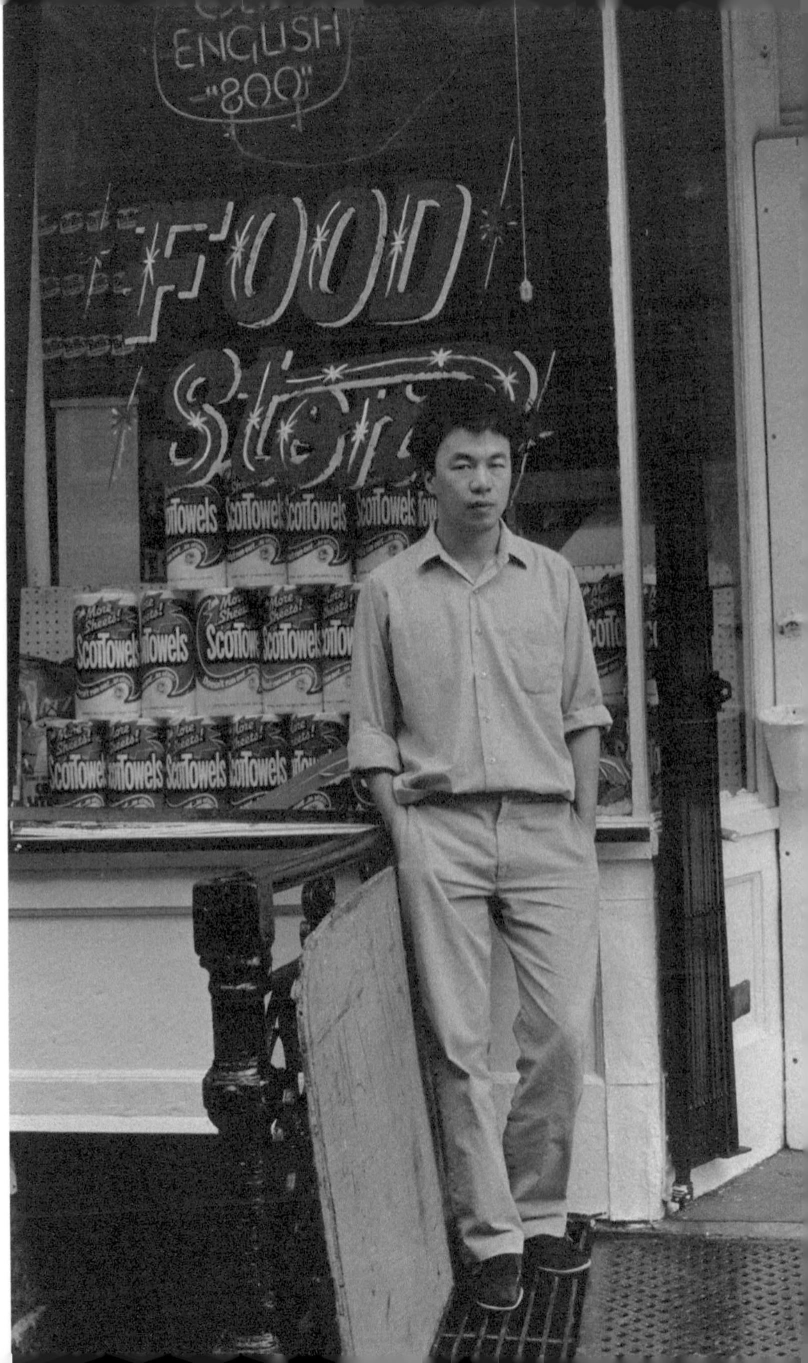
ENGLISH
"800"
FOOD
ScotTowels
More Sheets!

For this reason, I immediately grabbed the opportunity at that time and went to America. There, under completely different circumstances, a new chapter of refugee life began.

An existence between worlds creates a permanent feeling of estrangement.

It is neither comfortable nor truly liberating. It takes away all sense of security and makes you feel almost every day that a vast distance has developed between you and society and its culture. This gap cannot be transformed into a bridge merely by changing your circumstances.

MY MOTIVATION

Chapter 2.

Naturally, these experiences also influenced my art, which ironically I only noticed later. What I previously lived through was the only *experience* available to me. Other forms of influence had yet to emerge, so I didn't even have the option to relate to *different* perspectives. That's also something to keep in mind when people today, from a position of superiority, reproach refugees—stranded in the middle of nowhere—for not being "flexible" enough.

Every human being is a product of their environment, and lucky is the one whose horizon of experience has a chance to expand early on.

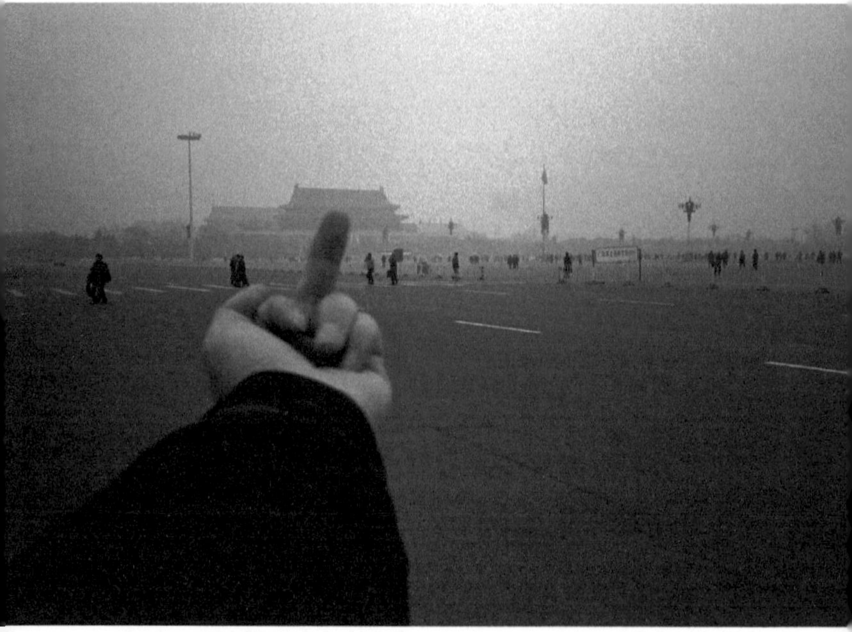

My own life demonstrates this. Even before I was imprisoned in China—though I was already aware of the threat of being arrested, I wrote notes in my blog. Among them was one about jealousy.

In truth, I was always jealous of my father because he had been in prison and I hadn't. I was jealous because I thought that, unlike him, I would never be able to survive something like that. That's precisely the point. Only when you learn to understand and articulate your feelings—including the abysses of fear and anxiety—do you begin to understand the core of what it means to be human. And suddenly, as if scales had fallen from your eyes, you realize what defines you—and, just as importantly, what defines everyone else.

You have to get to know yourself in order to develop trust in others—in recognition of our similarities.

But that is not easy. After all, we are not really taught *to understand* one another.

Perhaps this is also why there are so few people who have seriously delved into the refugee crisis. Who takes it upon themselves to visit 40 camps and interview approximately 600 people? Yet, I want to truly understand the things that interest me.

I seek out new experiences, connect them with previous ones and try to understand. I wouldn't even call it work—it is *life* itself: searching for answers and seeing whether there is something I can do.

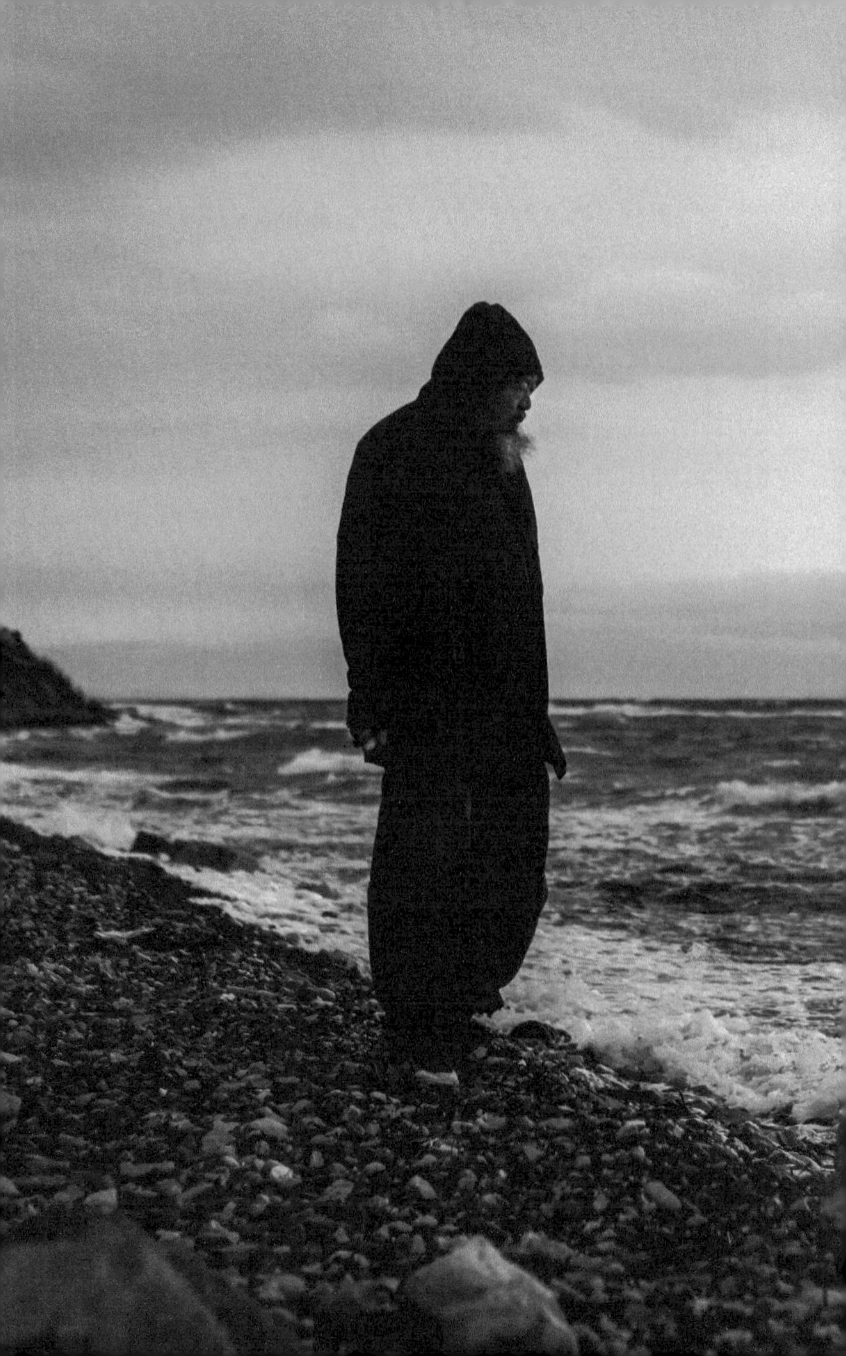

For you yourself are changed, too, when you see a child whose eyes till reflect the horrors of war and a potentially deadly escape across the sea. And so, my present self still remains directly connected to that young boy from long ago, who received his earliest and most formative experiences in a remote Chinese village. This is how my worldview was formed.

The question, of course, is whether one can even find words for something like this. I am an artist, not a writer. For a long time, I did not have the ability to verbally express such feelings of alienation—and this too connects me with the alleged "muteness" of today's refugees, their silence and hesitation when questions are fired at them, whether by journalists or officials.

The ability to speak needs its own time and a kind of calm space, where life experiences can be transcended.

Only once you have mentally detached yourself from the immediacy of a particular event and, over a longer period, made other experiences as well, will you be able to articulate your feelings with precision. This is why I only began writing and posting online after 2005, gradually gathering up my experiences again. That marked the beginning of something new—a written discourse.

What is art?
For me, it is
synonymous with
transmitted experience.

It can take on many different forms; it is a long, often winding, and sometimes tortuous process. Still, all of my efforts move exactly in that direction; they are linear. It is like traversing a mountain or crossing a river: We always only know the stretch that already lies behind us.

On the path still ahead, we might well encounter an abyss or a set of rapids, but of course, we don't know that yet. What might lie on the other side of the mountain remains unknown to us—even if we have already reached the summit.

So one must continue onward, full of curiosity—especially *because* our individual life, just like the era of the human species within the universe, is extremely limited.

Nor are there any guarantees in the process—but this, too, must be endured. Both the chance and the risk, indeed even the threat—all of this is part of life and of art; neither can be had without it.

If I insist that human rights are universal, it may at first sound abstract.

Yet, the opposite is true; there is nothing more concrete than accepting the simple truth that these rights are an expression of innate human needs. Who wants to live in fear, be tortured and discriminated against?

Far from being a "Western invention," the question of human dignity and the protection of inherent *rights* concerns us all.

Ultimately, all this also safeguards us from the destructive potential that lies dormant within us. Without such protective mechanisms, there can be no free– and not even a relatively stable–society. Some in the West actually believe these protections apply only to themselves, but that is by no means the case: the fact hold true not only for Western Europe, but also for Asia, for Middle East, Africa and Latin America.

And because it pertains to every human being, it pertains to all of humanity.

All these *innate* needs—
for fairness, for justice,
for freedom of speech,
for a fulfilling life—have
existed long before me
and will continue to
persist when I and my
generation are long
gone.

That, then, is continuity. And at the same time, every day is a new day, full of new experiences and new sentiments. As an artist, I try to find expression for this—verbally or non-verbally.

The refugee movement posed particularly great challenges for me in this respect. What form, what language, what genre is appropriate to describe what we are now witnessing?

From internet notes to installations up to my film project *Human Flow*, I have tried all kinds of approaches to find an answer—but I am still on the way.

In the process, my environment has also changed. For example, at some point after my arrival in Germany, the local media discovered that I am not the previously imagined hero who merely opposes a dictatorship. Since then, there has been hardly any media coverage about me.

It is actually quite an interesting misunderstanding: something was projected onto me that I am not—or at most only partially am.

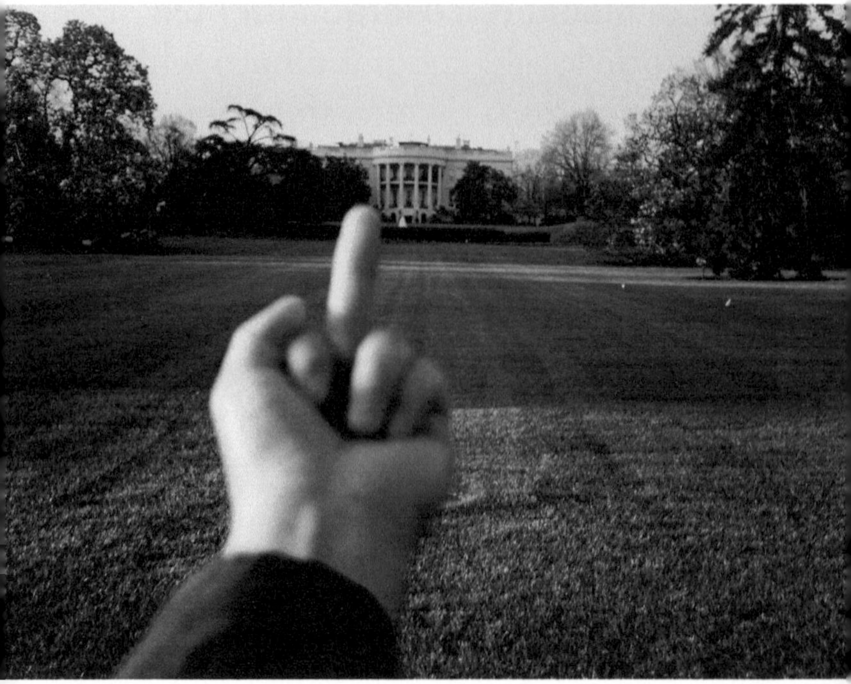

However, what I resist, what I fight against, is in fact far greater than any given dictatorship. I resist all ideologies that strangle a society—against stupidity, against narrow-mindedness. Because unfortunately, these evils are universal.

WHY PEOPLE FLEE

Chapter 3.

Being a refugee is a fundamental anthropological constant. It has been proven that there is not a single developed society that did not at some point have to move, or that didn't come into being as a result of migration and arrival.

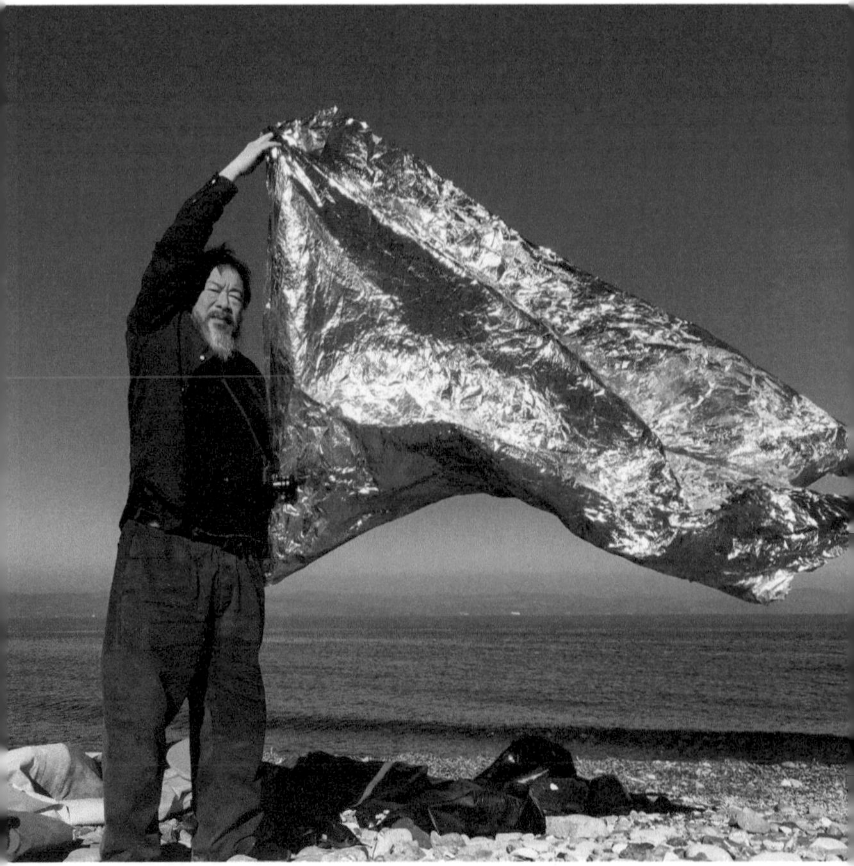

The ability to adapt to new environments and to overcome all of the difficulties that humankind has faced since time immemorial is perhaps the most important characteristic of our development as individuals and as a society. In fact, it's not always about *flight*, but also about *movement*—and the two often merge into one another. However, I do not wish to idealize this in any way; this millennia-old phenomenon has frequently led, and still leads, to war and the displacement of others.

Still, regardless of how we view it, mobility—and the opening up of new possibilities for choice—is an integral part of human culture, for better or for worse. Ultimately, it is up to us to determine what we make out of it and what boundaries we choose to set.

In all of this, we all too quickly forget that nations themselves are a relatively new concept. They only emerged late in the span of human history. I see them as something temporary. Here, too, development will continue—especially since has long since become clear that

nations are not necessarily always forces of freedom, but very often are also destructive and strangle the very people they are meant to serve.

Let's delve a bit deeper into the topic.

It's not only dictatorships that behave in this way. Even a state that is internally structured more or less democratically is not immune from committing large-scale atrocities.

These arise from the advantages that such a state creates for itself—even over undemocratic, economically less efficient states. The motivation behind such harsh conduct is rarely rooted in a political ideal; rather, it stems from a basic human drive for acquisition and dominance.

Even allegedly democratically legitimized power here relies on the law of the jungle. And while a certain order may prevail internally, setting limits on the barbaric aspects of human nature, this order is then, so to speak, “outsourced”—to the detriment of countless people in other countries.

Many of those who suffer elsewhere now are now streaming to the West. I do not mean to claim that Western countries are responsible for every malaise that happens elsewhere. But let's return to the fundamental point: human rights are indivisible. For this is what connects refugees, across all times and places–the search for precisely those very basic fundamental rights. Incidentally, this also connects them with those who are not refugees, despite all national, religious, ethnic, sexual, or generational differences.

In the entirely realistic recognition that every human being is created with the same rights lies an immeasurable yet very concrete opportunity for establishing peaceful coexistence within society. Put more simply, one could even call it a "win-win-situation."

But what must be done to achieve something so positive? Perhaps we should begin by abandoning certain categories that regrettably shape our thinking and actions all too much.

All too readily, we divide refugees into those fleeing war and persecution and those who have allegedly left their homes "only" for economic reasons.

Yet, there is something deeply arbitrary about this convenient distinction. And it is almost always inaccurate.

In how many cases does so-called "economic migration" actually result from political oppression!

It is provoked by corrupt and unjust societies, by the feeling—or rather, the experience—of being completely without rights, with not the slightest hope of even minimal social advancement.

So, what, then, do these people do?
They try to protect their lives and seek a better future for their children.

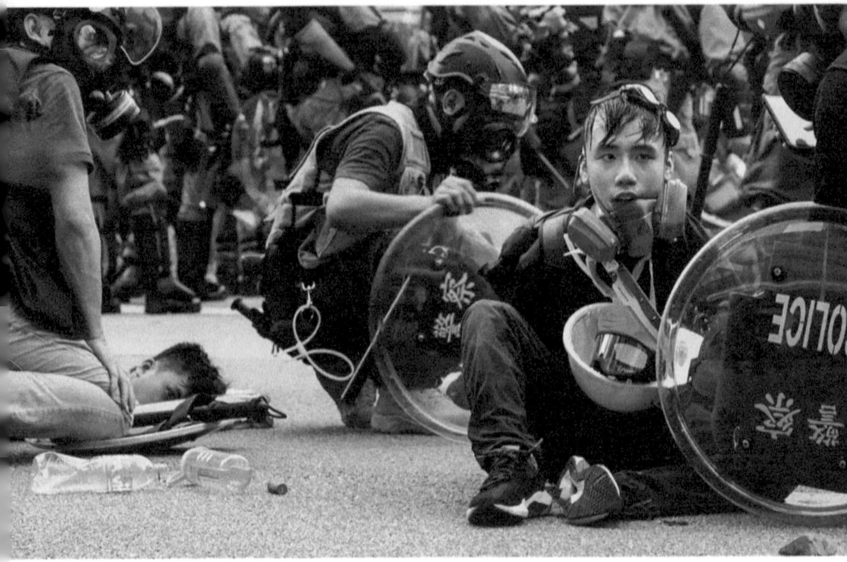

Question:
must a bomb first
fall on your house
before you
count as a
“real” refugee?

None of us should accept such a requirement. War is merely the last and most radical phase of social injustice—but even its many earlier forms can already be deadly.

This is precisely what we must not close our eyes to. Especially because to this day, politics continues to operate with the aforementioned, thoroughly artificial distinction—

as a notorious tactic for avoiding responsibility. At best, it is evidence of a staggering lack of imagination and understanding of human nature.

For let's be honest: Who would take on the burden of telling their children "We have to go" and clenching them under their arms, if not provoked by the direst of emergencies? People who are well-off stay at home.

Who, then, really believes that refugees are risking the dangerous journey simply on a whim?

According to some politicians, protection-seeking refugees are classified somewhere between terrorists, homeless people, and beggars. Hoping to win votes, these politicians thereby instill fear and undermine society.

At the same time, there's probably within each one of us a kind of primordial fear of the unknown—and with it, an instinctive desire to shut others out. That's why it is so important to confront and reflect on this—and to recognize that our resentments and phobias are actually shared across generations.

Throughout history, there has been no shortage of attempts—to withdraw and shut oneself off, just as there has always been courage in the face of death, and human ingenuity in escaping from hostile environments. Borders were erected, ditches dug, banks raised, and walls built—manifestations of brutal force, a kind of extension of war.

Borders are the concretized refusal to communicate and to understand the other side. That's why borders often merely reinforce sheer ignorance and bear witness to the inability to perceive what is actually happening behind them.

China, for instance, possesses the greatest and longest wall of all time. Its construction was commissioned by the first Chinese emperor, Qin Shi Huang Di, who at the time was a virtually all-powerful ruler. This happened more than 2000 years ago. From a purely physical point of view, this wall remains an extremely impressive construction even today. However, at no point in history has it been able to prevent a foreign invasion. In the meantime, its significance is exhausted in its existence as a world-famous tourist attraction that feeds a whole host of tourist guides and souvenir vendors. That is all.

In contrast, the original intention of the then emperor to keep people out has long since become an anachronism. I will gladly repeat: The wall has not achieved this goal–it has, plain and simple, *never worked*.

All the piled-up stones should have protected against intruders and conflict, but what actually happened? Bloody wars continued to be fought—many even *within* its own borders. It is therefore ridiculous to believe that one can box in all the ambiguities of human behavior by simply erecting physical barriers. It is one of our most fundamental misunderstandings about the nature of human beings—a convenient evasion.

In the meantime, it is the United States that is falling into this self-made trap and is on its way from being a magnet for refugees to becoming a fortress. At least this seems to be the intention of the current administration, whose entire politics reveals a fundamentally negative disposition toward refugees.

This won't last. A nation can only endure in accordance with its own nature, and fortunately we know: Migration and the USA have always been bound together—they are virtually one and the same. And since every action by an individual or by a society contradicting its own nature is doomed to fail, this most recent chapter about building a wall will likewise end in disillusionment. What wasted energy—energy worthy of a better and more promising cause!

Of course, the concerns of the local population—the descendants, whether recent or distant, of previous refugees and immigrants—must be taken seriously. Even here it is beneficial to reflect more deeply and weigh the issues more carefully than the usual hysteria stoked by some politicians and the media.

That's why we should ask ourselves: What does stability actually mean? Is it really by accident that economically prosperous and dynamic societies define precisely this word in terms of an on-going challenge not to let social inequality become too great? This is something quite concrete and can be seriously discussed on a case-by-case basis. However, when states like North Korea, Russia, or Cuba repeatedly and ostentatiously speak of "stability," they probably mean something quite different. But what truly protects a society: rigidity or flexibility?

I believe that even this example shows how important it is to think critically, compare, and weigh things carefully before using such complex terms.

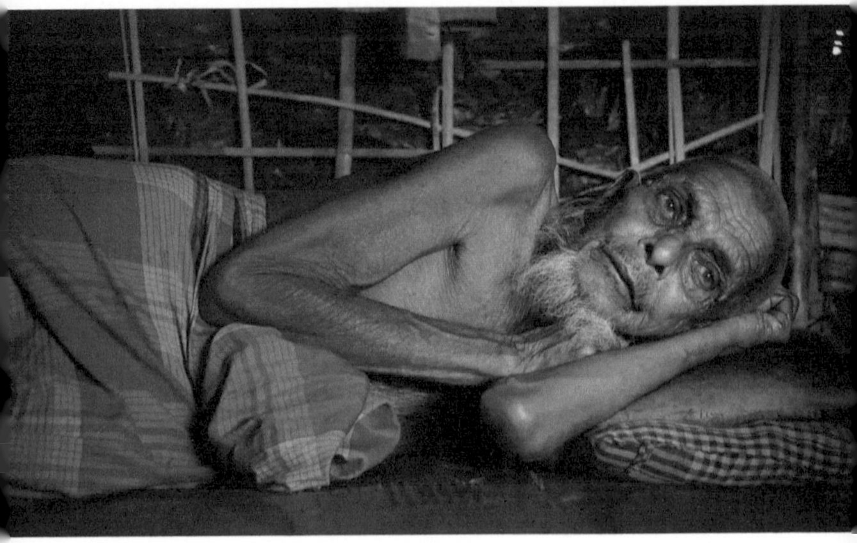

To view
so-called
foreigners
as a burden
or even a danger
merely paralyzes us.

Anyone who has previously taken on the existential risk of flight will, in all likelihood, go on to be a dynamic part of any society—provided that society is willing to engage with them and help create a common future.

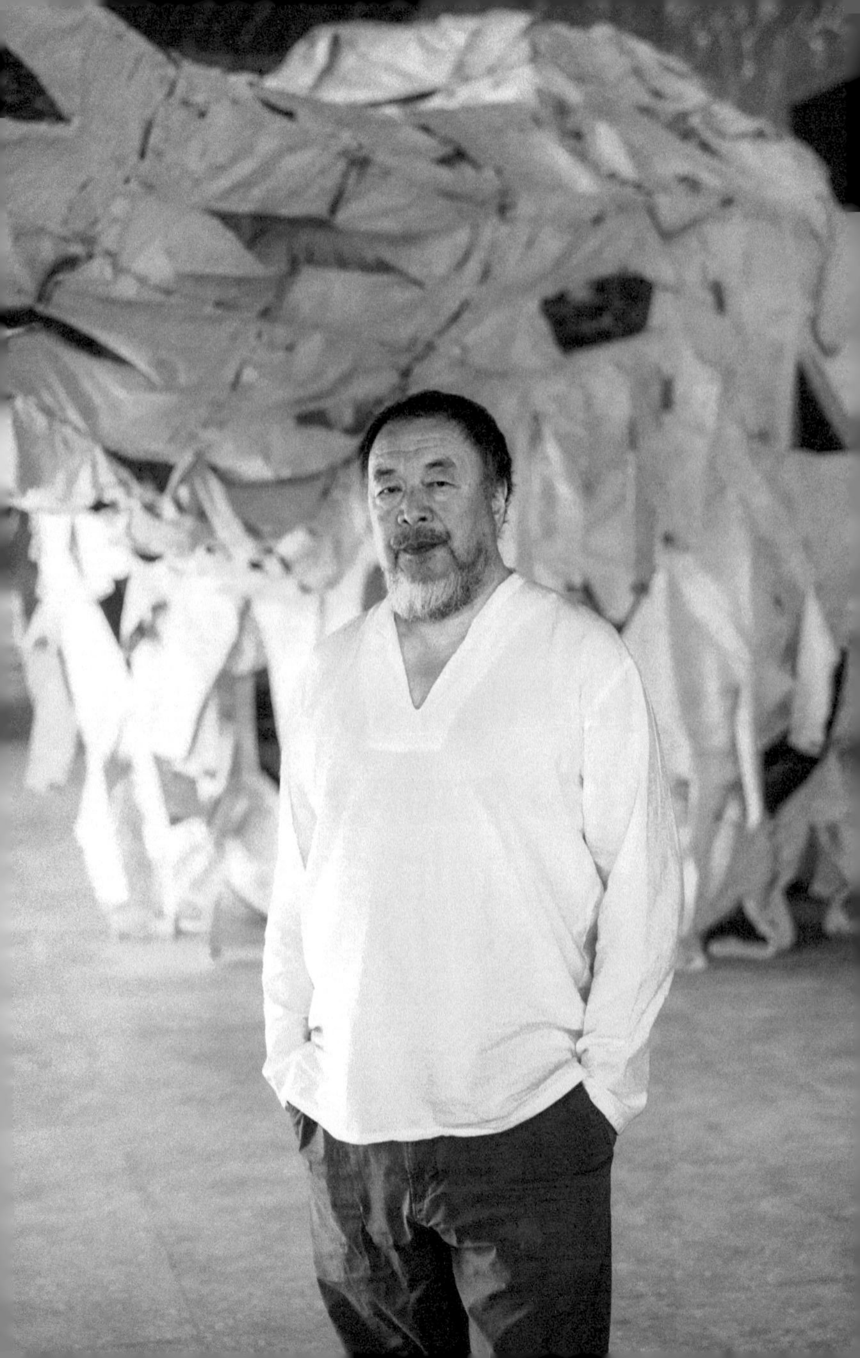

In fact, motivated refugees and immigrants—as history has shown, from the Huguenots in Germany to Germans and Asians in America—can even become a more vibrant part of the social fabric than the already established groups.

This must be kept in mind again and again—as a return to tradition in an intelligent way. Only in this way can one ultimately motivate and integrate, so that it benefits society as a whole.

Given all that, what would then be my task?

I describe it moderately: It is about opening up a space for imagination, beyond the old tracks of ideology and resentment.

That requires time as well as a language that is neither rushed nor dictatorial. And it requires trust in the goodwill of others, no matter who the other may be in any given situation.

At the same time, one's own privileged status should not be forgotten.

After all, not everyone has the opportunity and good fortune to devote a large part of their time to contemplation.

However, this insight should not lead to ineffectual pity, but to concrete responsibility.

MY ACTIONS
Chapter 4.

I have been filming documentaries for many years. In China, they dealt with social injustice, but this only touched on a quasi-first layer. What has always concerned me are the deeper layers beneath the surface. That's why I have developed a working method of immersing myself in unfamiliar situations—documenting and investigating them to get closer to the heart of the problem.

As long as my eyes are calibrated *for it* and my mind is still able to ask questions, my camera will always keep running.

At the beginning of every project, of course, there are enormous technical and logistical obstacles to overcome. A team with the right people must be assembled, equipment needs to be obtained, accommodations planned—all of these things. But above all, you must be willing to move on, through boundaries and across borders—both geographical and mental. In the case of *Human Flow*, there was the additional challenge of even getting permission to access all the refugee camps. In every country, at every camp, the process began anew. And because I was filming in various continents, I encountered a wide range of different political systems. Bureaucracy was present everywhere—and in some places there were also very real physical dangers. But even these can be managed, as long as you are determined not to give up.

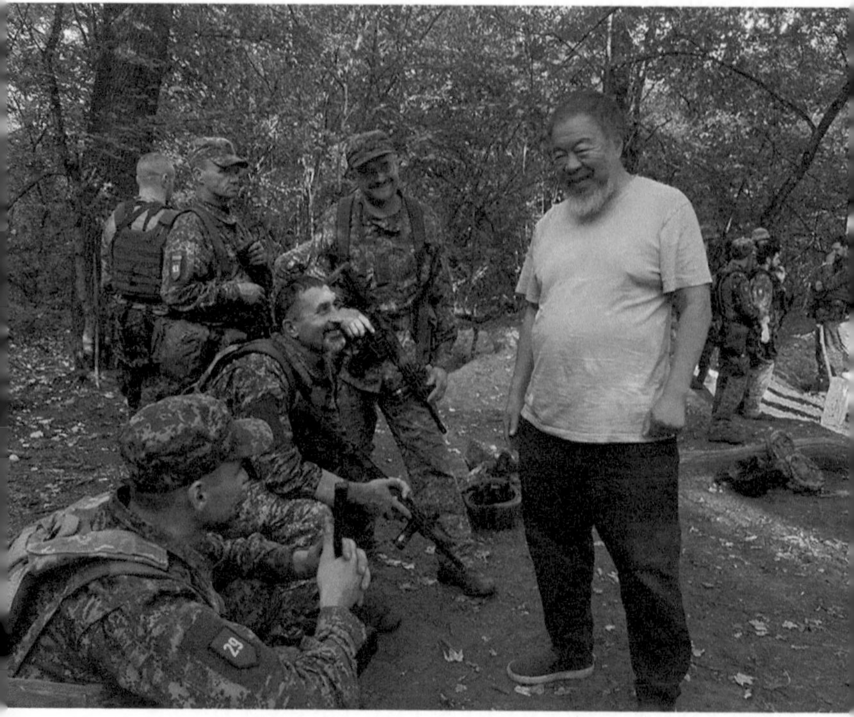

Or perhaps even more importantly, once you begin to understand that this very violence is one of the reasons *why* you're making the film in the first place.

I definitely did not confront all of this unprepared—respect for such a profound subject demands as much. As early as 2014, when I was still in China, my team and I had already begun our research. My studio assistants flew to an Iraqi refugee camp and spoke with the people there. In addition, a foundation had asked me to look at some drawings created in one of the refugee camps.

From that point on, I worked towards assembling a team to visit these places and document what was happening there through interviews. Shortly afterward, I received my passport and was able to leave China.

And what a coincidence: This happened at exactly the moment when over a million refugees were arriving in Germany and being taken in. This gave me the unique opportunity to approach the topic in a way that I had never envisioned before.

Had I not been in Berlin at the time, I would certainly not have been able to engage so deeply with all of these realities and fates. Above all, I wanted to find out why these people had left—or *had* to leave—their homelands. But why would a man who had just arrived from China, of all people, want to talk about refugees? This made some people in Germany skeptical, even suspicious. Was this perhaps just self-promotion, or even a bid for attention?

I didn't respond to that. But I did ask myself: If there was any truth to these suspicions, why isn't everyone who wants to be famous engaging with the refugee issue? What still holds true to this day: It would make me very happy if more people got involved with this problem.

At that time, my partner and our son had already been in Germany for a while. The mother of a classmate of my son, who is a doctor, had volunteered to help take care of the newly arriving refugees. When I finally came to Germany, I immediately told myself: You also have to get to know these people. This is why I made the decision to make the extensive documentary film that was released in 2017 under the title *Human Flow*, with a running time of 140 minutes.

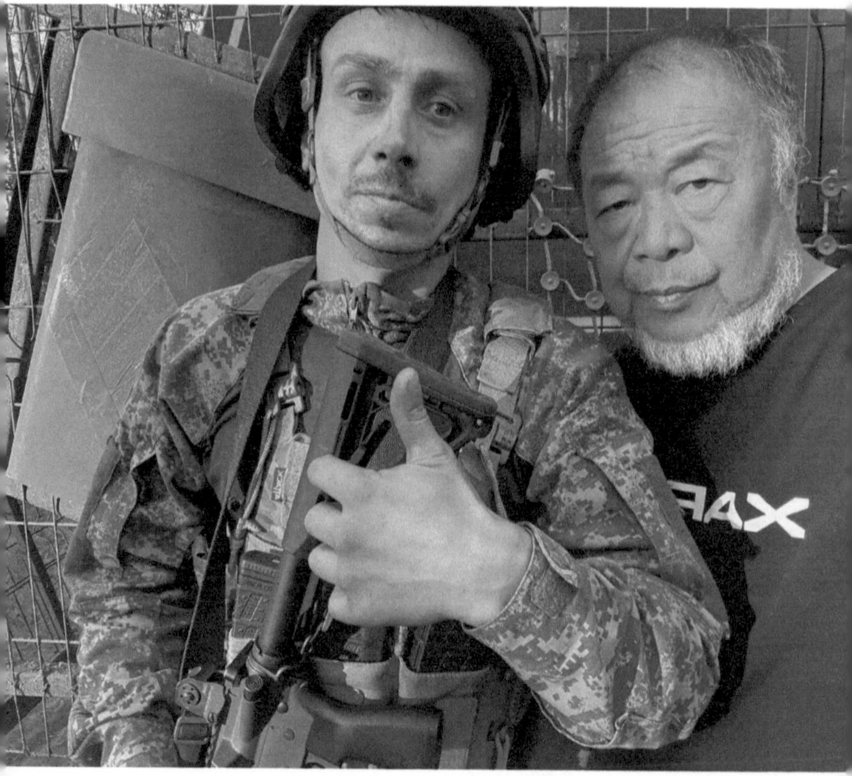

In the summer of 2015 we traveled to Lesbos. My eleven cameramen and I then filmed approximately 900 hours and conducted hundreds of interviews—from Myanmar in the East to Mexico in the West, from Kenya in the South to Berlin in the North. We visited 40 refugee camps, each accommodating a vast number of people. The more we learned about them, the more clearly a certain texture began to evolve.

Their individual stories were strikingly similar and, in their sheer number, merged into one single narrative of almost unimaginable scale. We wanted to try to understand this phenomenon: This is not just about one poor boy or one needy family—it is about a major event in human history, nothing more and nothing less.

My approach is consequently a global one, which is the reason for our allegedly zigzag itinerary between camps and continents. According to UN figures, approximately 70,8 million people are currently in the process of fleeing—more than ever before. Concretely, this means: All these people were forced to leave their old lives behind, get into boats, travel across seas, endure month-long travels by foot through deserts and mountains, often in climatically or socially hostile environments. They experienced immense suffering and deepest despair, many witnessed the deaths of those closest to them.

This is what I wanted to learn more about.

So, I tried to approach these streams of refugees from two perspectives: from above, using drones to film refugee camps and crisis regions; and from below, as an observer who asks these fleeing people questions, talks and eats with them, and yes—even dances with them.

Let us therefore go back to the beginning one more time—back to Lesbos, the first stop in my film.

Every European is surely familiar with the name of this Island—not least thanks to the Ancient Greek poetess Sappho. One could say it is a core part of the collective societal memory. Lesbos, of course, lies near modern-day Turkey and refugees have always arrived there. Yet even so, for me as a Chinese person, it was nevertheless a shocking sight:

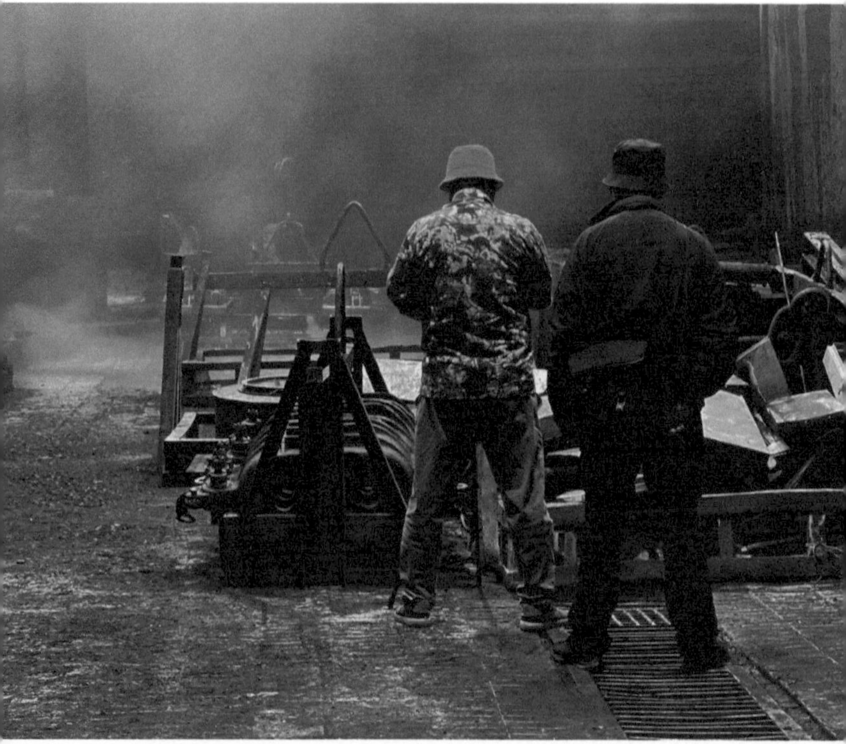

To see utterly exhausted people staggering out of tiny boats onto the shores this idyllic island, often helped by volunteers trying to assist them. These were refugees fleeing from the Syrian Civil War.
When you really see something like that—when you allow what you experience to truly sink in and become a lived experience—then one thing becomes absolutely clear, no matter what xenophobic populists may claim: Anyone who flees their homeland on one of these boats, escaping war, destruction and mass murder, wants—first and foremost, just one thing—to survive. And then to simply catch their breath again, in relative safety. Maybe, though, this existential need is bound up in an illusion: That Europe, as a continent of abundance, freedom, and democracy, will alone provide them the opportunity to stay and build a new life.

The reality, however, is different. Even today, the camps on Lesbos are hopelessly overcrowded, while Europe tries to punish the refugees and get rid of them by sending them back to Turkey. They all had hoped to escape war and find peace in Europe. Instead, they faced *deportations*. And here I am only talking about Lesbos—not even mentioning the Italian island of Lampedusa, or about the thousands of Africans who have died in the Mediterranean.

As a human being, as a citizen, but also as an artist, I *have to* therefore ask myself how I deal with such experiences of suffering, in order to make them transparent and to convey something essential to my contemporaries.

Unfortunately, we live in an extremely fast-paced time, in which one news story chases the next—if they are truly news at all and not merely sensations or, even worse, *fake news*. Our minds and nerves are brutalized by this and have become increasingly insensitive to the fate of other people.

Nevertheless, we must not allow ourselves to become discouraged or ever lose faith in the truth. Precisely because we see facts being distorted and even in the midst of democratic societies brazen lies emerging, we must continue to insist on accuracy. And we must strive to lead by good example, each of us in own way.

Along such a path, we come to learn something new about ourselves. Take, for example, these refugee camps. Are they not, inadvertently, a model of our own society? Do they not reveal how we perceive others and evaluate their lives? That's why I quite consciously opted for filming with drones—to make our generalized perspective visible, our crazed obsession with "having an overview."

And then, from there, immediately return to the people inside the camps, sitting in their tents whose tarps had been torn apart by the wind. Or crouching on the ground, which rain, storms, and catastrophic sanitation had turned into quagmire, and sometimes even a cesspool.

The question of the perspective is, in any case, not a merely technical one: Again and again, I've had to ask myself in what way and by what means to approach the truth—or rather, reality. It's not enough to simply "take a look at" it: What one sees also needs an adequate and clear narrative in order to be communicated to others.

I believe artists are in a better position to contribute more here than those journalists compelled, under great time pressure, to deliver "the right images" along with brief comments.

I will give an example. At the end of February 2016, our film crew arrived in Idomeni, that infamous camp on the Greek-Macedonian border. Up to 14,000 people were eking out an existence there without any support, on a cold, muddy field. At the same time, hundreds of the international press had already gathered there. Their numbers had swelled so much that suddenly they themselves became a part of the story, something newsworthy in their own right! That's absurd. With one foot, they stood in the rain and mud of the camp; with the other, in the hallways of their mainstream media corporations.

It's therefore hard to say whether the information and the voices they were able to "capture" in Idomeni were really apt to raise social awareness among viewers.

With all due respect for these reporters, I was—and remain—rather skeptical. The manner *how* the reporting was done was very superficial, often leaving out important background information, failing to talk about the causes that forced the refugees to flee, and with routine speed, made every tragedy look the same. It is not that lies were told—some journalists were genuinely empathetic. It's therefore hard to say whether the information and the voices they were able to "capture" in Idomeni were really apt to raise social awareness among viewers.

Still, as always, the same mechanism played out: Either the media reported far too much about something, soon leading to saturation and indifference, or they didn't report at all. That is why I found most of the coverage paralyzed—and paralyzing.

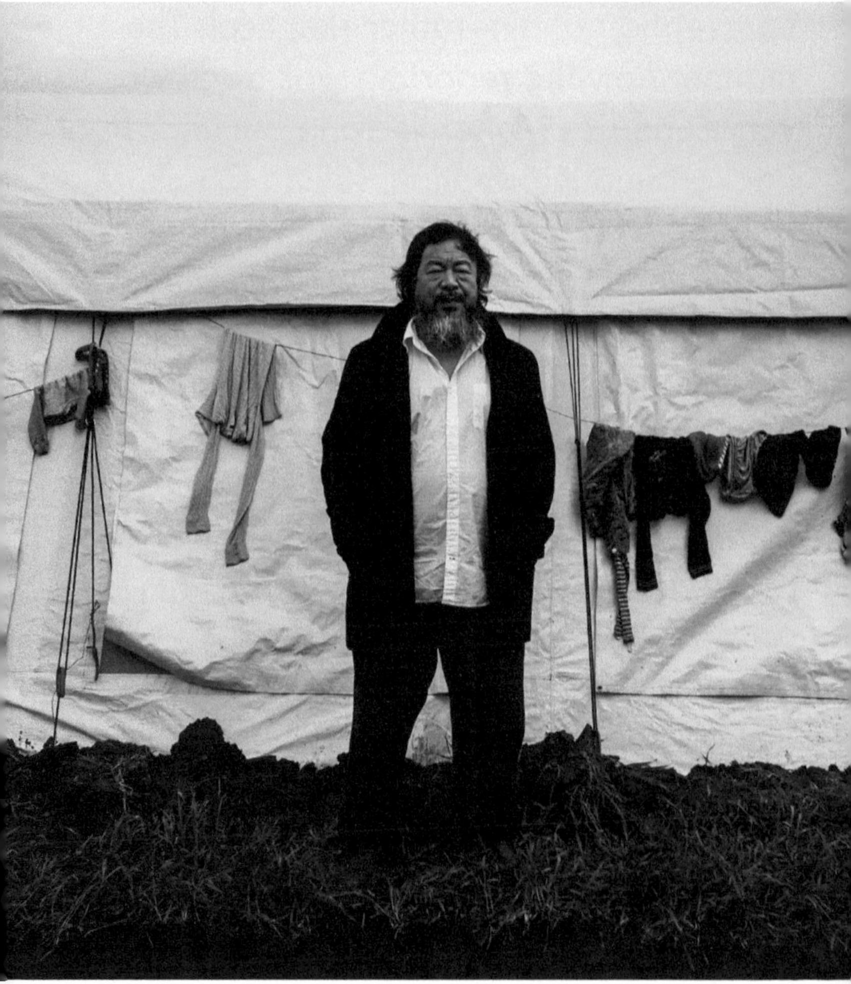

Despite the best of intentions, it revealed our collective helplessness in the age of modern media. Although the media are perhaps not as modern as one would like us to believe.

Even in Idomeni I was searching for a different approach.

We wanted to find authentic, personal stories, not interchangeable stereotypes.

This is why ten to fifteen people from our team stayed on site for months until the camp was dissolved—right up to the moment when all objects left behind were cleared away and disposed of.

We took many of these objects-turned-garbage with us, washed them, and now display them in exhibitions.
For even inanimate objects, such as clothing, shoes, fragments of mirrors, combs, razor blades, blankets, or SIM cards, communicate something; they evoke the homeless, dislocated part of human biographies and make us pause and reflect.

MY SUMMARY

Chapter 5.

I am well aware that my performances and actions might seem ridiculous—or somewhat comical. But they are not posed, nor a performance—they stem from genuine interest. I am not a detached historian but a human being and an artist. I want to connect with what moves me and create something out of it.

In theater, there is the figure of the jester who makes the king laugh—a funny, absurd, or humorous character that comments on events that would otherwise have an excessively heavy effect. Such figures bring the spectators back to the actual story. For me, the primary focus is on people and their shared humanity. I witnessed the worst of what humans are capable of at a very young age. But that is not the whole story. One must not stop there, must not let one's worldview become rigid.

Later on, and continuing to this day, I found that people are eager to tell me about themselves, examine themselves and open up. This happens completely naturally, without the slightest psychological manipulation. And it is inspiring! Because, once again, in the process, one inevitably learns a great deal about oneself.

After all, I am neither better nor different from all those people forced to flee—I am one of them. *This* is what I want to convey: It is our mortality and constant vulnerability that connects us with one another.

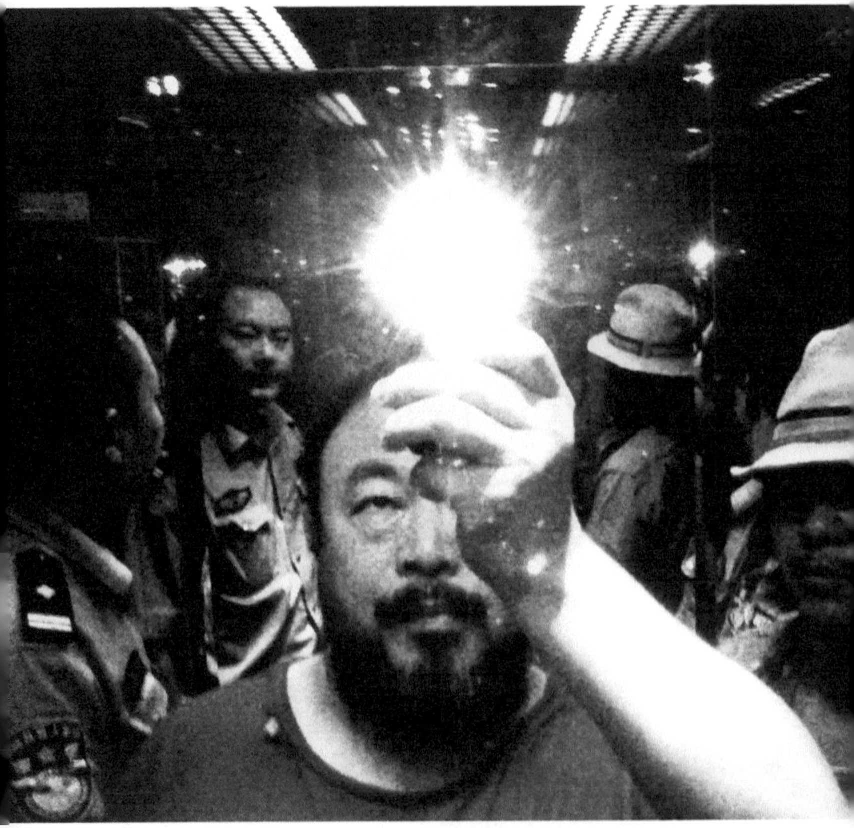

I am more than 60 years old now, and my life could be over quickly. I could disappear off the radar tomorrow—who knows? Naturally, I am as afraid of that as anyone else; I am just as vulnerable as all of us are. Why we are born, and when and why we depart—these remain the greatest mystery of our existence. That is why I try to enjoy the splendor of life—just as we all try to do.

The only thing that we can really do is share our warmth and passion with others.

Beyond the personal, it is above all art that can touch and transform people who seem foreign to each other—sometimes it can even bring them together. As an artist, I am therefore required to work with all my senses.

The challenge is great, so I must develop an authentic language. The wrong approach would be to latch onto the success of someone like Arturo Giacometti and suddenly start making only thin sculptures because they sell well.

Every single artist constantly redefines their means and forms of expression; that is what makes art so valuable, but also so fragile.

Artists transgress borders every day in order to find their own voice.

For it is a fact that the world is made by individuals. For me, this means:

Art can change the world! If we allow ourselves to keep dreaming and imagining, then anything is possible.

Art is extremely important because it reaches individuals—both those who benefit from politics as well as those who are harmed by it. In the end, every political decision harms or helps *individual* human beings, not just abstract demographic figures.

If we believe that there is a place within every human soul for sincerity, kindness and compassion, then art can reveal this most precious aspect of life—our vulnerability as human beings. This idea stands at the heart of my film about refugees, as well as my entire working philosophy.

Why? Because I believe that I must share my modest notions of humanity with others. It is about communication and empathy. First and foremost, it is a matter of giving a voice to the people living in these camps and tents, who often cannot even get a cup of hot tea. Because I believe that this can give them at least a bit of hope. To state it clearly in conclusion:

If an artist is not an activist, they are a bad artist. Art must define values and create meaning. Art has always been a realm of activism when it comes to questioning consciousness and moral judgment.

The refugees' path could be a driving force for civilization. If we allow it, it will enrich our minds, our knowledge, literature, visual arts and music. Our lives become more colorful through the *Human Flow*: it sets society in motion and makes it overall much more interesting

This is why I don't view what is currently happening all over the world as an apocalypse, as the xenophobes in every country try to make us believe every day, but rather as a profoundly human, flowing movement.

People have always fled, from the beginning of humankind. It is almost as natural as the movement of water, wind and grass.

I do not wish to romanticize this in any way—after all, water and wind can also be brutal and destructive. Just like the human beings, who are currently destroying the environment in a suicidal manner.

For this reason, I can also understand the other side. If you own a beautiful house with a lovely garden, and then suddenly a strange neighbor moves in, and then another one comes—who might even bring along their relatives—you become afraid. We humans, after all, are pragmatic beings.

Our moral and religious convictions, our God, and our notions of evil have all arisen from our own needs.

It all has to do with how we humans think and act. Germany, for example, has gained moral credit through its engagement with history and its responsibility for World War II. It has proven itself to be a responsible country with strong principles.

But why are these principles so strong? Because after the war, most Germans were convinced that they had to invent themselves anew, that Germany should be a country looking toward the future. For a short while, this is why Angela Merkel—as then US President Barack Obama said—was on the right side of history. And yet, Germany's admittance of so many refugees was not motivated purely by humanitarianism.

Germany is the driving force behind the idea of European unity, and as such the country had hardly any other choice but to act as it did, since the refugees were already in Europe. Greece and Italy had reached the limits of their capacity to take in refugees, and the continent had not been this divided over an issue in a long time. In this respect, the relief felt in Germany after the negotiated "Turkey-Deals" was understandable. From then on, it no longer had to shoulder the burden alone, as that would have led to enormous new political problems.

And yet, this doesn't mean that, from a broader historical perspective, anything has truly been gained.

The question that remains is this: What kind of "solution," are we actually talking about and for whom? Only for Germany? For Europe? Or for the entire world community? And could Germany, on its own, be able to come up with a rational solution to the problem? Of course not. China, Russia, and all other leading nations would have to take part.

We need a truly visionary plan. For every one of us can do something—either slam the door in the refugees' faces or open it for them. We have a choice, and I advocate for trust and for returning dignity back to these people.

Borders exist so that they can also be torn down.

As an artist, I am constantly stumbling upon them: There are aesthetic, philosophical, and also social borders that can restrict my work. I have to question them, just as I must question myself. Of course, this is a challenge, and it sometimes leads me into desperate situations. But I must do it, or I would feel as if I had given up.

And what would my son think of me? He should remember his father as a fighter, someone who always held on to his convictions.

When my film was finished, I asked myself: And what do I do now? I had the feeling that I was once again left empty-handed. But then I told myself: Actually, it's enough to keep reminding people about the refugees. What they need most is not money but to be seen as human beings. This respect for them can consist of very little—a short report in the news, or telling one's own child: "Please finish your meal. There are 70,8 million people, many of whom did not have breakfast this morning."

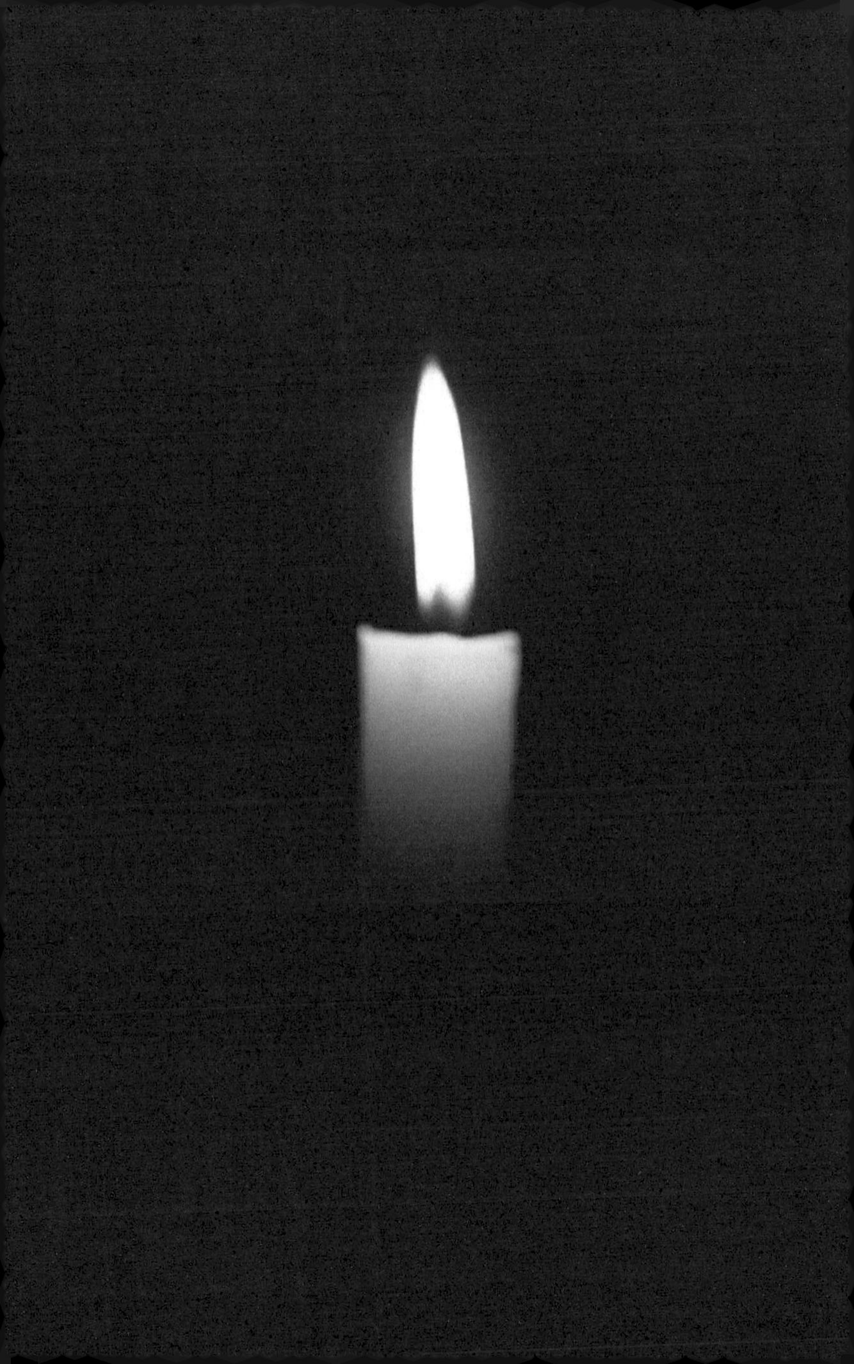

Anyone who feels no shame becomes part of the darkness.

But everyone can light a candle.

And in its light, we discover how much of what we separate in our thoughts and actions is actually interconnected. If I have managed to awaken even a sense of this, perhaps the purpose of my small *Manifesto without Borders* has already been fulfilled.

p. 14: Film still from Human Flow, 2017
p. 28: Ai Weiwei and Ai Qing at the 852 Farm, Heilongjiang Province, China, 1958
P. 36: Qalandiya Checkpoint, West Bank, 2016
P. 40: Selfie by Ai after the return of his passport, July 22, 2015
P. 46: Ai Weiwei in Williamsburg, Brooklyn, 1983
P. 52: *Study of Perspective - Tiananmen*, 1995-2003
P. 56: Ai Weiwei on Lesbos, 2016
P. 74: *Study of Perspective – White House*, 1995-2003
P. 80: Ai Weiwei on Lesbos, 2016
P. 94: Film still from *Cockroach* (2020)
P. 112: Film still from *Rohingya* (2020)
P. 116: Ai Weiwei in front of *Three Perfectly Proportioned Spheres and Camouflage Uniforms Painted White*, Kyiv, 2025
P. 126: Ai Weiwei with Ukrainian soldiers in Kharkiv, Ukraine, 2025
P. 132: Ai Weiwei with a Ukrainian soldier in Kharkiv, Ukraine, 2025
P. 138: Ai Weiwei in a train factory in Kyiv, Ukraine, 2025
P. 152: Ai Weiwei in Idomeni refugee camp, 2016
P. 162: *Illumination*, 2009
P. 186: Candle lit in memory of the students who died in the Wenchuan earthquake

Ai Weiwei

Ai Weiwei (b. 1957, Beijing, China) leads a diverse and prolific practice that encompasses sculptural installation, filmmaking, photography, ceramics, painting, writing and social media. A conceptual artist who fuses traditional craftsmanship and his Chinese heritage, Ai Weiwei moves freely between a variety of formal languages to reflect on the contemporary geopolitical and sociopolitical condition. Ai Weiwei's work and life regularly interact and inform one another, often extending to his activism and advocacy for international human rights.

A global citizen, artist and thinker, Ai Weiwei moves between modes of production and investigation, subject to the direction and outcome of his research, whether into the Chinese earthquake of 2008 (for works such as *Straight*, 2008-12 and *Remembering,* 2009) or the worldwide plight of refugees and forced migrants (for *Law of the Journey* and his feature-length documentary, *Human Flow*, both 2017). From early iconoclastic positions in regards to authority and history, which included *Dropping a Han Dynasty Urn* and a series of middle-finger salutes to sites of power, *Study of Perspective* (both 1995), Ai's production expanded to encompass architecture, public art and performance. Beyond concerns of form or protest, Ai now measures our existence in relation to economic, political, natural and social forces, uniting craftsmanship with conceptual creativity. Universal symbols of humanity and community, such as bicycles, flowers and trees, as well as the perennial problems of borders and conflicts are given renewed potency though installations, sculptures, films and photographs, while Ai continues to speak out publicly on issues he believes important. He is one of the leading cultural figures of his generation and serves as an example for free expression both in China and internationally.

Ai Weiwei has exhibited extensively at institutions and biennials worldwide, including at Seattle Art Museum, Seattle (2025);

MUSAC, León (2024); Design Museum, London (2023); Albertina Modern, Vienna (2022); Serralves Museum of Contemporary Art, Porto (2021); Kunstsammlung Nordrhein-Westfalen, Dusseldorf (2019); Oca – Ibirapuera Park, São Paulo (2018); Public Art Fund, New York (2017); Israel Museum, Jerusalem (2017); Palazzo Strozzi, Florence (2016); Andy Warhol Museum, Pittsburgh (2016); National Gallery of Victoria, Melbourne (2015); Royal Academy of Arts, London (2015); Martin-Gropius-Bau, Berlin (2014); Brooklyn Museum, New York (2014); German Pavilion, 55th Venice Biennale, Venice (2013); Hirshhorn Museum and Sculpture Garden, Washington DC (2012); Taipei Fine Arts Museum, Taipei (2011); Turbine Hall, Tate Modern, London (2010); Haus der Kunst, Munich (2009); Mori Art Museum, Tokyo (2009); documenta 12, Kassel (2007); and Kunsthalle Bern, Bern (2004).

Ai Weiwei's architectural collaborations include the 2012 Serpentine Pavilion and the 2008 Beijing Olympic Stadium, with Herzog and de Meuron. Among numerous awards and honours, he received the Praemium Imperiale for sculpture from the Japan Art Association in Tokyo in 2022, won the lifetime achievement award from the Chinese Contemporary Art Awards in 2008 and was made Honorary Academician at the Royal Academy of Arts, London in 2011. His human rights work has been recognised through the Václav Havel Prize for Creative Dissent in 2012 and Amnesty International's Ambassador of Conscience Award in 2015.

The artist's memoir *1000 Years of Joys and Sorrows* was published in 2021, and his autobiographical graphic novel *Zodiac: A Graphic Memoir*, in collaboration with Elettra Stamboulis and Gianluca Costantini, was published in 2024.

Ai Weiwei lives and works in Beijing (China), Berlin (Germany), Cambridge (UK) and Lisbon (Portugal).

ISBN: 978-3-96258-231-9

1. Auflage 2025 PalmArtPress, Berlin

Original title: MANIFEST OHNE GRENZEN

This publication was printed on FSC-certified paper
using a carbon-neutral process, supporting sustainable
forest management worldwide.

Layout: NicelyMedia
Hergestellt in Europa

PalmArtPress
Pfalzburgerstr. 69, 10719 Berlin
www.palmartpress.com